To Breathe

Melanie Duncan

To Breathe

Acknowledgements

Previously published:
'Matthew' and 'I Am Mother' in *Looking Through the Glass,*
Ginninderra Press, 2006
'Child', 'Autumn', 'Tuxedo Sunset', 'Freedom', 'Surveillance',
'The Recipe' and 'Wings' in *To While Away*, Ginninderra Press
Pocket Poets, 2017
'A Wilderness' in *Wild*, Ginninderra Press, 2018

To Breathe
ISBN 978 1 76041 933 2
Copyright © text Melanie Duncan 2020
Cover photo: homecare119 from Pixabay

First published 2020 by
GINNINDERRA PRESS
PO Box 3461 Port Adelaide 5015 Australia
www.ginninderrapress.com.au

Contents

To Breathe	7
Seashells	8
The Stars in the Sky	9
A Piano That Plays	10
The Nullarbor	11
Melting Trees	12
The Crackle	13
To Labour	14
In My Excitement	15
The Question of Freedom	16
The Transformation	17
The Caterpillar	18
If I Cradle	19
The Apple Pie Exterior	20
The Water	21
The Reset	22
For Mandy and the Sunshine	23
Moulded Into	24
Listening to Vivaldi on a Rainy Day	25
The Enchanted Garden	26
The Aftermath	28
A Chinese Lantern	29
The Question Mark	30
The Dusk	31
Saturday Night	32
The Fish	33
Thursday Afternoon in Brisbane	34
Words	35
The Heart	36
The Schoolmaster	37

If Words Could Suffice	38
The Commuter	39
I Still Remember	40
The Moon	41
The Corsage	42
The Disassociation	43
The Gentle Rain	44
Paranoia	45
For You	46
Kite Flying	47
The Artist	48
On Reflection of *Dubuffet's Right Eye* by Bill Brandt	49
We Are Alive	50
Memories	51
A Wilderness	52
Matthew	53
Child	55
Autumn	56
Tuxedo Sunset	57
Freedom	58
Surveillance	59
The Recipe	61
I Am Mother	62
Wings	64

To Breathe

The words
Must breathe
In birdsong and ease
Or convey
Every breaking sun.
The lyrical soul
Is an aperture of beauty.

Seashells

Watch the array of shells and rocks
I collect in bare hands,
As I bathe each one
In waters of blue;
I bask in the noon sun
As the light radiates
Their glistening hue.

The Stars in the Sky

Flying my kite in the nonchalant air
Of a sinking sun,
I will bargain with the wind
And elevate my line
To illuminate each word
For the stars in the sky.

A Piano That Plays

Keys rise in unison
In ivory attire
Stirring in the light.

They bow and rise
So gallantly
In the rapture of the night.

In interlude they lie
Extolling the tempo
Of the beat.

Tenderly they touch
And seek
My fingers' playful reach.

The Nullarbor

The road stretches ahead
Where streaks escape into dusk,
Melding the edge of a star spun sky;
Nullarbor to Nowhere.

Banks of dirt and saltbush
Intersperse the edge.
Suddenly a lone camel appears,
Is it real or a mirage?

But there is only a piercing road
And the long, drawn-out gasps
Of a thousand voices
That echo in the husky wind.

Melting Trees

Trees are melting to the ground,
Blackened and charred.
The forest becomes bitumen
And simmering concrete.
It boils and bakes,
As I drive,
I wonder where am I going?
As my windows fog and steam up,
My vision blurs
And I cannot see.

The Crackle

Watch the crackle in the air,
The underlying bite,
The friction in space
When one of them strikes.
Verbal sparring
In Soho, Ipswich or Bladewood,
Everywhere
But not here now
And she forgets
When she is alone,
As his hand
Imprints her heart;
Moulding her chambers
With indelible marks.

To Labour

Rivulets of sweat
Are dripping in his eyes,
Parched and thirsty
Beneath the melting sky.

Smoothing the surface
To dry so evenly,
No fissures or cracks
He surveys so keenly.

He can only heed
To the dictating ground,
As the concrete dries too quickly
And the sun beats down.

The water bottle beckons
But is still a walk away,
The concrete is unyielding
For this he has no say.

In My Excitement

In my excitement,
I would catch tadpoles
In the waterbeds
And puddles
Of my youth
And carry them home.
I would lie in bed
And listen to their cries,
As they jousted
In the rain.
Their guttural 'ribbets'
So deep and pronounced,
Such a pandemonium
And uproar;
But now when I listen
I hear no sound at all.

The Question of Freedom

The border sits staunch and defined
As our flag ripples in the breeze,
The question of freedom
Is contemplated
On the encumbered ground.
Her teardrops fall
Into pools
Of transparent puddles
Which reflect
The sun,
Distinct and beautiful
But steadfastly apart.

In Nauru
People cry and whisper,
'Emancipate our lives
Don't leave us here
Indefinitely,
See past this shelter and bed;
For today
Is another day
Humanity
Might transcend.'

The Transformation

Seeds parched and thirsty
Are nestled within
Moist particles
Of soil.

They showcase
Their stems
As they posture towards
Sunlit clouds
Of pink hues.
They waver and stretch
Towards the cotton candy
Of buoyant blue.

Infantile tomatoes
Are cradled
Within
Integuments
Of thickening green,
As each fruit
Transforms from yellow
And orange
And into a sun kissed
Red.
They emerge into
Delicious mounds
Of circular flesh.

The Caterpillar

The caterpillar
Threads through
Shrouds of leaves
Before settling
In repose.

Cocooned inside,
The butterfly
Awakens,
To break
The girth
Of its
Chrysalis.

Manifesting enchanting
Wings of
Ochre and honey,
It flutters by
Whilst I am unable
To close my eyes.

If I Cradle

If I cradle a green leaf
In the palm of my hand,
Subdue the ice and lessen the rain,
Take a breath
And alternative seasons transpire
To coarsely imitate
The beauty of now;
I could forget
How this moment exists.
The leaf curls so gently
Nestled within,
So delicate and profound.

The Apple Pie Exterior

Photoshopped an image today,
Retweet or resend?
A caption to deliver
All apple pie exterior.
Never mind the good, old
Buttery crust,
Air brushed for the good:
(Think aesthetics).
The paradigms are shifting
Appropriate to the mood.
Realities are
Debatable
And may also be
(What?)
Unfavourable.

The Water

The water is a myriad of life,
Majestic and vast,
A slice of heaven
To revere;
Swallowing up
The falling drops
Of our lonely tears.

Blue and translucent,
This solitary jewel
Inspires us to overcome
The desolation
And waste;
Placating our feelings
Of sorrow and hate.

It still beholds,
Far from only
A mirror for the sky;
As it reflects and winks
Its scintillating eye.

The Reset

There is an emptiness,
A void to be filled,
A gaping space.
As she forgoes her sense
For the ecstasy of now.

I see each page falling,
Ripped and torn;
A visage of rainbows
Dulling and blurring
In the aftermath of now.

She hears his voice
But cannot see,
Tonight she will reckon
On her own
Before she breathes.

For Mandy and the Sunshine

Girl with hula,
On a beautiful day;
The hula whirls,
Cutting the air
In fervent circles.

Girl twirling a hula
On a windy day.
The beach is high,
Romping against
A backdrop of blue.

Girl spinning a hula,
The hula pulses and plays
To a vista of
Scintillating shades,
Mesmerising
This winter's day.

Moulded Into

Careful what she says…
The words rock inside.
Clenching her hands,
Everything is fine.

Twisting from the inside,
The misshapen corset
Fires up now,
Deciphering a turbulent line…
A shallow voice
Escapes in time.
Groaning within
The rocket blasts aloud…
Constraints bursting,
Lace and stays all round;
Sparking into potent flames,
Combustible and angry,
Expressing herself
With a
Gut-wrenching sound.

Listening to Vivaldi on a Rainy Day

The Four Seasons of Vivaldi
Serenades the air,
Bestowing violins
To stir each heart;
Soothing and lulling
Each soul
Crumbled in pain.

We can seek the sky,
The powder blue that makes us sigh,
The streaks of red
Congealed and thick
And the flickering light
That transforms itself so bright.

As the music builds
To rapturous height,
This concerto of 'Spring'
Implores a belief
And expectation
Of all such
Fortunate things.

The Enchanted Garden

Roma Street Parkland, 2017

A canopy of trees,
Adorned by garlands
Of abundant leaves,
Framing the picture
Of a starry night;
Bespeckled by the glow
Of fluorescent lights.

Waters flowing and cascading
In projections of colour.
The elevated images
Court the moonlight
In iridescent light.
The vibrant glow
A homage to the night.

The children run and play,
Their fairy costumes
In nonchalant disarray.
Brimming in joy,
Mischief and hope,
Circling the grass
And jumping rope.

I see the twinkle and shimmer
Of bulbous globes
Illuminating every flower,
As I meander through
Majestic trees
I feel so calm
And such peaceful ease.

The Aftermath

He smokes not far from the sea.
His family are his backbone
Strength and dignity.
He can bury his wounds
In the recesses of his mind
And in moments of lucidity,
He can sometimes abandon
The war's epiphany.

But when wracked with pain
And his knuckles are white
And he can barely will his eyes shut
In the middle of the night,
His family will seek
To alleviate and hold
And they warm his hands
When he feels the cold.

A Chinese Lantern

The sounds echo
Reverberating around,
As red paper
Is laid;
Each page is folded
In delicate shapes.
They softly breathe,
As each word
Fights through slits
Exquisite and narrow;
To animate inside
This Chinese lantern.

The Question Mark

The reservation of the words,
Heavy and weighted.
A cliff's edge
Into a blue abyss,
The uncertainty
Quivering inside.
The seagulls flock
And jubilantly cry,
As they parade their feathers,
Soaring together
In glints of white.
They eye the distant shore
As the esplanade shrinks,
No need to wonder why.

The Dusk

Scarlet rays
Throw a glance
Of indifference,
As clouds are spun
And the light fizzles
Through the embers
Of a dying sun.
The shadows stain
Roofs and arches
In burgeoning contemplation
Of a sombre view.
The only sight
Brightening the dusk
Are feathers of vivid white,
As each cockatoo
Alights to preen
In defiance of the night.

Saturday Night

Strumming a guitar
On a Saturday night,
Music and company
Align to form
The perfect interlude.
We can trace the
Boundaries of the stars
While he sings the blues.

The Fish

Streams ripple
Through the wind,
As fish sparkle
Poetic flashes
Of metallic silver.
They vie for the attention
Of our animalistic urges
To capture and contain.
They whirl past
Like colourful sirens
Luring our senses,
As we gravitate to the thrill
And exalt in the chase.
Their steadfast eyes
Sharply incise,
As they teem
Through rippling waters
Of cyan blue;
They defy and counter
Our resolute moves.

Thursday Afternoon in Brisbane

My happy place,
An emporium
In brocade and velvet
Is draped in
Champagne lace.

An afternoon diversion
Of pebbled stone
And architecture,
Where the well heeled
And tired and grumpy
Traverse
The pavement;
As exuberant scooters
Fly by
I drink in
Their captivating faces.

Words

Words can hurtle,
Like explosions
That catapult
From familial cloth.
They ricochet
Damage and bruise.
The entrails are left
To slowly bleed,
As his exterior
Hardens
And turns to
Stone.

The Heart

Captivate her heart,
When dawn slowly breaks,
She may breathe contentment
When bruised by your smile.

Captivate my heart,
As our insight evolves
I may slowly break
When I relinquish my hold.

The Schoolmaster

Bursts of spontaneity
Refresh like the breeze,
As far flung bags
Intersperse the school
And peals of laughter
Erupt from jovial students
Stealing moments of relief.

They were oblivious
To the advance
Of the schoolmaster.
His striding steps
Were measured and intent
Focused
On reaching his mark.

If Words Could Suffice

If words could suffice
And somehow endeavour
To make it all right,
We could click a button
Like a robot
(Except we're not robots).
We are all human,
Each of us carry
Our shattered hearts.
Some pieces are blunt
And are made hardy
Through time and age,
Other fragments still pierce,
Lacerating with stealth,
Exposed and dangerous
Like broken glass.

The Commuter

The commuter
Silently watches
The bustle of people
Arch in time,
Milling in crowds
Just like clockwork.
As the pendulum swings
His hands unclench…!
The cool, fresh air
Is an impromptu relief.

I Still Remember

I still remember
Each song you sang,
Your patience
As you would take
Your time.
Lost in your eyes,
I turned towards
The warmth
Of a brighter sun.
I held your hand
As my heartbeat quickened,
Uninhibited
Beneath a slow-moving
Kaleidoscopic sky.

The Moon

I will climb
The gentle incline
And upward sloping cliff,
Though the trees will seem to
Swallow me
Into some glorious
Finality.

Each tendril encompasses
The beating of my heart,
As well as the rising pinnacles
And far reaching summits.
I will rocket through to
The far corners of the moon
Just to elevate the night.

The Corsage

Notations
On careless sketches,
The marks
Familiar almost endearing.

Textures
On a weighted canvas,
The ink marks are brushed
On a silverpoint etching.

Scented papers
With private musings
Are clutched to her heart.
The light is shining
On her fashioned corsage.

The Disassociation

Too tired I am…too tired,
I have always pushed
What if I now float?
Too late I see
I have missed
This padded quality.
This soft, thick eiderdown
I could slumber on.
The shiny faces
And well-meaning voices
May all dumb down.
Here I am
Not asleep…not fully aware,
A kind of
Rapturous
Disassociation;
Not here
But at a distance
I can comfortably
Bear.

The Gentle Rain

I could see
A shadow fused
To a thickening haze,
Eclipsing the
Crimson sun.

Our buds were maturing
In their unique way,
Pitched in pairs
Swallowing up whatever
Moisture the weather would share.

What's that you say?
'The mark was unmet
And so therefore we object.'
'Never mind! Never mind!
We have lifted our eyes.
Awareness comes from within
And I cannot fathom to obey
Following in such a way.'

No applause…no reprimand
I will cup my hands
Towards the tenuous drops
Of the gentle rain.

Paranoia

The cat stalks the air
In her paranoid ways.
Her eyes wide open,
As the groaning wind
Blows hollow
From her ravenous belly
And crumbly leaves
Descend and fall.
Taut and rigid
She springs into action,
Her sharp claws spear
Without hesitation.

For You

I have fractured my own heart,
As I have bled
Drops of red…
Rivulets of consternation
For you
And I would
Again.

Kite Flying

Shining orbs lit every kite,
Afloat and dancing,
Their strings in step
To a wandering breeze.

Their colours melded,
In fans across the sky,
Like luminous rainbows
Alive with fire.

The Artist

His fingers caress
The soft covering
Of fine moss,
As leaves line
Intricate pockets,
Brushing pale undertones
In swaths of lime;
Like an artist
Subtly imprinting
A lichen face.

His eyes wrinkle in
Contemplation,
As he mellows
And softly hums.
I see
An old man's
Cliff face,
Smiling through
The glistening drops
Of transparent dew.

On Reflection of *Dubuffet's Right Eye* by Bill Brandt

An image of an eye
Is captured yet alive.
His wrinkles crease in
Formation
Like patterns in the sand.
Deep furrows lined
In detail,
His story intricately
Marked.
Dubuffet's Right Eye
On a photographic print
Stares
Unabashed and glassy,
Forever now enshrined.

We Are Alive

Alive! Alive!
I see you are alive.
A tourniquet is sought
From the cloth that I fashioned,
Your wound can be bandaged
And the bloody drips lessened.

Alive! Alive!
I am alive.
The air is perfumed
With eucalyptus and scents,
Filled with the hewn stems
Of scented primrose remnants.

Alive! Alive!
We are alive.
Clasping each other in passion as one
Mutually bound together and fused,
Tonight our heart string rhythms
Will orchestrate love and infuse.

Memories

Her memories
Are filtered through…
Infused and steeped
In cinnamon and honey.
Just a teaspoon here
And twisted tight
To suffuse the light.

Her glass jars
Are secure yet fragile,
But prone to break
In fragmented parts.
She refines today's selection
From the larder of her
Recollections.

A Wilderness

A wilderness
Overwhelms my soul
Unleashing its tremors
And irregularities,
Forming awareness
Of soft frailties
And wonderful complexities;
The heights and summits
Of pulsating ecstasies.

I breathe through
The tides of anguish
And plummeting depths.
The soft meanderings
Induce peaceful rest
That soothe and relieve
My weary soul.

I climb and soar
Each tempestuous peak,
Returning within
To where my heart beats.

Matthew

I was sitting down with muddled-up thoughts of what to write.
My eldest son interjected my thinking with:
'Write a poem, Mum, of Matthew's disobedience and how he
Always starts the fights.'

My ginger-haired son smiled at me through his golden freckles
And spots,
His bright, blue eyes shining.
Mischief was etched all over his face with a capital M exclamation
Mark, dot.

This cute little threesome had emptied my drawers
Demolished my jewellery, hidden my bag
And sawed off my lipstick while he coloured my walls.

What to do? A smack, bribery or perhaps he should be sent to his
Room?
Discipline and work, I feel so strung out.
I muster up some energy as I relegate him into the room of gloom.

Fifteen minutes passes… 'Mum, can I come out?'
'No, you stay there for another ten minutes.'
The music plays in my ears. As I half close my eyes, I see
Matthew sneaking about.

Should I do something or pretend I didn't see?
Will the world change so much
If I pour myself that other cup of tea?

Mmm…the aroma fills my senses.
I stop, look out the window. I feign shock, surprise.
'Matthew, what are you doing on top of that fence?'

'Look, Mum!' he beams brightly. 'See what I can do!'
He executes a perfect back flip,
His actions diverting me from the punishment due.

I march Matthew back inside, still erringly unable to see.
Patrick has been quietly reading his book.
'You know, Mum, next time you should write a poem about me.'

Child

(For Patrick)

I hold your dimpled hand,
Your hair nestled upon my breasts.

I will breathe upon your sails
And paint your sky.
It must be blue and nothing else.

The glass will not shatter,
Each star its own heaven;
Question marks to emblazon
Your eyes.

Autumn

Autumn's breath will slowly freeze,
Reflecting light
To mock and tease,
The icy grass
And hunchback trees.

Wounded forms of rotting wood
Are shrinking from decay.

I see a staunch tree,
A throne for cockatoos
To alight without care.
Parading snowy plumage
To exalt upon the air.

Tuxedo Sunset

The faces stand out
Like an apparition from my twenties,
The grandeur
And parties and buoyant hope.

The fine dresses
And tuxedos
So cutting in masculine pride;
The dances we shared
And laughter we sought
In pursuit of the sun.

Now wiser and measured
I remember the ridiculous,
I draw on those times
And remember
I want to
Still make it mine.

Freedom

Pale light diminishes
Through shrouds of clouds,
As dusk settles
Poignant and thick,
On mountains crowned
By haphazard stars.

Figures traverse
Through paths
Both worn and secretive;
Not erring in their journey.

Their footsteps freely walking,
Their beating hearts yearning
For a sanctuary.
They trail the slopes,
To climb rocks and dirt
Happening upon a place;
Possessing and guarding
A private haven
Where freedom awaits.

Surveillance

Abandoning technology,
I stand and sigh.
Hands unclenched
Relishing the light,
Releasing tension
And focusing eyes.

The air circulates
In spontaneous gusts,
Unbidden and free.
I walk slowly
In absolute leisure,
No buttons, devices or clicks…
Recording aborted
In a delirium of bliss.

I can capture the moment,
Freeze the image in my mind
To replay over and over.
The contrasts and shapes
And punctuating sounds
Intoxicating and leisurely,
I saunter in the midst
Of an oasis so heavenly.

Solitary and alone
Now if only I could…
I see the moon has risen
And the night is bleak
From the impulses that fight
To entangle and keep.

I peel back the layers
And listen for a click,
I blink my eyes once
As surveillance begins.

The Recipe

Do you think of me?
I wonder…
Marinating in melancholy sauce,
My blood, red heart icily torn apart
Still folding this memory for you.

I will slice the strawberries
Tenderly dust
And coat with sugar.

I will cradle you in my arms
If only to indulge,
Caress you in passionate tides,
Envelop you in warmth
And garnish lost time
In forget-me-nots.

I Am Mother

My voice vibrates through you
As clothes hide my burgeoning waistline.
You are nurtured within the warmth of my body,
Suspended in a reservoir of wonder.

Bonded to my surrounds,
You sense my movements and exalt in my voice.
Cloistered in a private haven,
Secure in my nourishment.

Suddenly you are restricted,
Involuntary spasms begin then falter.
Space narrows as you are confined.
My body is torn in agony
As you inch forth.

Now light surrounds,
As laboured breathing steadies.
Your blue eyes vivid and defined,
Receptors to shadows which merge and fade,
I cradle you close.

You are swathed in cloth
And placed in your crib.
You touch the foreign, cold glass surrounding you
The smooth, clear walls silent and unyielding…

When you hunger…	I nourish you.
When you shiver…	I warm you.
When you tire…	I cradle you.

You snuggle your face in my warm, mounded breasts
And revel in our naked contact and fragrance of my skin.

I am Mother.

Wings

Beautiful things,
Fluttering wings;
Teasing languid air.

A pop and a crackle,
The air springs alive;
As flower beds sigh.

Petals grasp and reach
Filmy motions
Of transparent wings.

www.ingramcontent.com/pod-product-compliance
Lightning Source LLC
Chambersburg PA
CBHW062200100526
44589CB00014B/1887